ALL

Meat

Shabnum Gupta

New Dawn

NEW DAWN
An imprint of Sterling Publishers (P) Ltd.
A-59, Okhla Industrial Area, Phase-II,
New Delhi-110020.
Tel: 26387070, 26386209
Fax: 91-11-26383788: E-mail: sterlingpublishers@airtelmail.in
ghai@nde.vsnl.net.in
www.sterlingpublishers.com

All You Wanted to Know About - Meat
© 2004, Sterling Publishers Private Limited
ISBN 978-81-207-2650-5
Reprint 2007, 2009

All rights are reserved.
No part of this publication may be reproduced, stored in a retrieval system or transmitted, in any form or by any means, mechanical, photocopying, recording or otherwise, without prior written permission of the original publisher.

Printed and Published by Sterling Publishers Pvt. Ltd.,
New Delhi-110 020.

Contents

Preface	5
Glossary	6
Mutton	9
Lamb	73
Chicken	93
Fish and Seafood	133

Preface

The secrets of non-vegetarian food unfold in this unique collection of meat recipes. Easy to make, delicious to eat, each dish is enhanced with a subtle flavour – a sprig of coriander, a tang of spice or a sprinkling of cheese.

You will be amazed at the things you can do with ordinary mutton, chicken, lamb, fish and seafood. With these recipes, each meal will turn into a fantastic feast!

So go ahead and pamper your palate with these marvellous dishes!

Glossary

FRUITS and DRY FRUITS

Almond	Badam
Apricot	Khurmani
Avacado/Pear	Naspati
Cashew nut	Kaju
Coconut	Nariyal
Grape	Angoor
Mango	Aam
Pineapple	Ananas
Raisin	Kishmish
Walnut	Akhrot

VEGETABLES and LENTILS

Bean sprout	Anpurit saim
Bengal gram	Chana dal
Cabbage/Lettuce	Band gobhi
Capsicum	Shimla mirch
Carrot	Gajar
Cauliflower	Phool gobhi
Cucumber	Kheera
Eggplant	Baingan
Green chilli	Hari mirch
Green gram	Moong dal
Kidney bean	Rajma
Lady's finger	Bhindi
Lemon	Neembu
Onion	Pyaz
Pea	Matar

Potato	Aaloo
Pumpkin	Sitaphal
Radish	Gajar
Red chilli	Lal mirch
Spinach	Palak
Tomato	Tamatar

HERBS and SPICES

Ajinomoto	Chini namak
Bay leaf	Tej patta
Cardamom	Elaichi
Cinnamon	Dalchini
Clove	Laung
Coriander	Hara dhania
Coriander seed	Sukha dhania
Cumin seed	Jeera
Curry leaf	Curry patta
Fenugreek	Methi
Garlic	Lahsun
Garlic salt	Lahsun ka namak
Ginger	Adrak
Mint	Pudina
Mustard	Rai, sarson
Peppercorn	Sabut kali mirch
Poppy	Khus-khus
Saffron	Kesar
Sesame	Til
Tamarind	Imli
Turmeric	Haldi

MISCELLANEOUS

Butter	Makhan
Cornflour	Makki ka atta
Corn oil	Makai ka tel
Cottage cheese	Paneer
Cream	Malai
Flour	Maida
Groundnut oil	Moongphali ka tel
Honey	Shahad
Semolina	Sooji, rawa
Sesame oil	Til ka tel
Vegetable oil	Vanaspati tel
Vermicelli	Sevian
Vinegar	Sirka

Preparation

Meat stock *Makes* 10 cups

Ingredients: 1 kg mutton; 1 large onion, peeled and quartered; 1 large carrot, cut into strips; 2 celery stalks, cut into thirds; 2 large leeks, cut in half lengthwise; 2 bay leaves; 6 sprigs fresh parsley; ½ tsp dried thyme; 12 whole black peppercorns

Method: Place all the ingredients in a heavy-bottomed saucepan. Cover with enough cold water. Cook over a high flame and bring to the boil. Reduce the flame and simmer for 3 to 4 hours. Remove any impurities that rise to the top. After about 3 hrs remove the pan from the fire and keep aside for 10 to 15 minutes. Strain and use when needed.

Mutton

Cabbage Delight

Serves 6

Ingredients

12 large and tender cabbage leaves,
washed and blanched
½ kg mutton, ground
1 large onion, chopped
2 cloves garlic, 2 tbsp ghee
A handful of coriander leaves
1 capsicum, chopped
2 tomatoes, chopped
½ cup each of dry breadcrumbs and
beaten curd
4 hard-boiled eggs, shelled and sliced
2 cups cooked rice
½ cup grated cheese
1 tsp garam masala
½ tsp powdered cinnamon
Salt and chilli powder to taste

Method

1. Heat the ghee and fry the onion and garlic till brown in colour. Add the ground mutton and fry.

2. Add the tomatoes, capsicum, garam masala, cinnamon and breadcrumbs. Cook till the meat is tender. Remove from the fire, add the coriander leaves and rice and mix well.

3. Put a portion of the filling on the cabbage leaf and roll it. Use toothpicks to hold the ends of the leaf together. Repeat the same with the remaining leaves.

4. Place them in a baking dish, sprinkle the grated cheese, add the boiled eggs, and then the curd.

5. Bake in a moderate oven (19°C) for 20-25 minutes. Serve hot.

Chilli Mutton

Serves 4

Ingredients

1 kg ground mutton
1 cup red kidney beans
4 onions, chopped
1 capsicum, chopped
6 tomatoes, chopped
6 cloves garlic, chopped
2 bay leaves
2 tbsp each of cornflour and oil
2 tsp cumin powder
4 peppercorns
4-5 green chillies
Coriander leaves for garnishing
Salt and chilli powder to taste

Method

1. Soak the beans in cold water overnight.
2. Heat the oil in a pan and fry the onions and garlic till brown. Add the capsicum and cook till tender.
3. Add the chilli powder, bay leaves, peppercorns, cumin powder and meat. Brown the mixture and add 5 cups water and salt to taste. Lower the flame and cook for 45-50 minutes, or till done.
4. Meanwhile, boil the beans and when tender, add them to the meat mixture with the tomatoes. Stir for a while, then let it cook over a low flame for 10-15 minutes.
5. Add the cornflour (mixed with 1 tbsp water) and cook till the mixture thickens.
6. Serve hot, garnished with the chopped coriander leaves.

Cabbage Mutton

Serves 4

Ingredients

¼ kg mutton, minced
1 each of cabbage and cardamom
4 each of onions and red chillies
2 cloves
1" piece cinnamon
2 tbsp oil
½ cup grated fresh coconut
1 tsp each of lemon juice and grated ginger
1 tbsp coriander seeds
½ tsp turmeric
A few chopped coriander leaves for garnishing
Salt to taste

Method

1. Wash the minced mutton and keep aside.
2. Shred the cabbage, grind the coconut and chop the onions.
3. Heat the oil and fry the onions and ginger till brown in colour. Add the turmeric.
4. Grind the cloves, cardamom, cinnamon, coriander seeds and turmeric and add to the above mixture. Fry for 5 minutes.
5. Add the meat, pour half a cup of water, cover with a lid and cook over a medium flame.
6. After a couple of minutes, add the cabbage and cook till the meat is tender.
7. Add the coconut paste and cook over a low flame till done. Remove from the fire and add the lemon juice.
8. Garnish with the chopped coriander leaves and serve.

Shami Kebabs

Serves 4

Ingredients

1 kg mutton, minced
2 onions, finely chopped
100 gm Bengal gram
4 cloves garlic, crushed
1" piece cinnamon
2 cardamoms
4 cloves
3 eggs, beaten
1 tsp each of cumin powder and ginger
3-4 green chillies, finely chopped
3 tbsp mint leaves
1 tbsp raisins
½ cup chopped coriander leaves
Salt and chilli powder to taste

Method

1. Mix together the meat, garlic, ginger and 1 onion. Cook over a low flame, adding some water, till the meat is tender.
2. Grind together the cinnamon, cardamoms, cloves, green chillies, chilli powder, cumin powder, mint and Bengal gram and add to the meat.
3. Stir well and season with salt. Remove from the fire and set it cool.
4. Grind this mixture to a smooth, fine paste.
5. Add the eggs and mix well.
6. Add the raisins and mix with the paste.
7. Form the mixture into balls, flatten and deep fry till brown on both sides.
8. Serve hot with the mint or coriander chutney.

Shahi Kebabs

Serves 6

Ingredients

½ kg mutton, minced
10 eggs
1" piece ginger
4 cloves garlic
1 tbsp cumin seeds
¼ tsp turmeric powder
1 tsp coriander powder
4 cloves
¼ cup lemon juice
Oil for deep frying
Tomato and onion for garnishing
Salt and chilli powder to taste

Method

1. Grind the ginger, garlic, cumin seeds and cloves to a fine paste. Add salt, chilli powder and the coriander powder and turmeric powder to it.
2. Boil 8 eggs. Break the remaining two and beat them lightly.
3. Cook the minced mutton, adding some water. Add the paste, beaten eggs and lemon juice to it. Mix well.
4. Coat the hard-boiled eggs with this mixture and deep fry in the hot oil, until brown in colour.
5. Cut the eggs lengthwise and serve with the tomato and onion rings.

Eggplant Mutton Delight

Serves 4

Ingredients

6 eggplants
100 gm mutton, minced
1 onion, chopped
1 egg, beaten
1 tbsp breadcrumbs
2 tbsp oil
½ cup grated cheese
Salt, pepper and chilli powder to taste

Method

1. Cut the eggplants lengthwise into halves. Scoop out the pulp from the centre and reserve the shells.
2. Mix with the onion.
3. Heat the oil and fry the onion and eggplant pulp mixture till brown in colour.
4. Add the mutton, egg, breadcrumbs and salt, pepper and chilli powder. Cook till done.
5. Stuff the eggplant shells with this mixture and bake in a moderate oven (150°C) for 40-45 minutes.
6. Sprinkle the grated cheese and serve hot.

Mutton Apricot Biryani

Serves 4

Ingredients

1 kg mutton
½ kg each of onions and potatoes
A pinch of saffron, dissolved in 2 tsp hot water
½ kg rice, soaked for an hour
1 tsp garam masala
1 cup curd, ¼ cup milk
30 gm each of almonds, raisins and dried apricots
2 tbsp each of ginger-garlic and green chilli paste
2 tbsp ghee
Tomato rings for garnishing
Salt and chilli powder to taste

Method

1. Peel the potatoes and cut into long strips.
2. Boil the meat with the ginger-garlic paste in salted water. Remove when tender.
3. Slice the onions finely and fry in the ghee till golden brown in colour. Then add the garam masala. Add the potatoes, curd and stir well.
4. Add the milk, apricots, almonds, raisins and salt and chilli powder. Stir till the gravy thickens.
5. Add the rice and 4 cups water. Cover with a lid and cook over a low flame.
6. Add the meat and saffron to the rice when it is semi-cooked.
7. Serve garnished with the tomato rings.

Spinach Mutton

Serves 4

Ingredients

½ kg mutton
1½ kg spinach, coarsely chopped
1 onion, sliced
2 tomatoes, chopped
1 tbsp curd
½ tsp cumin powder
1 tsp each of turmeric and coriander powder
1 tsp garam masala
2 tbsp ghee
1 tbsp crumbled cottage cheese
Salt to taste

Method

1. Cut the mutton into small pieces.
2. Fry the onion in the ghee till it turns pink.
3. Add the meat pieces. When they turn brown, add the chopped tomatoes, turmeric, garam masala, coriander powder and cumin powder and salt.
4. When the gravy thickens, add the curd and mix well.
5. Then add the chopped spinach and mix well. Cover with a lid, lower the flame and cook till done.
6. Serve hot, garnished with the crumbled cottage cheese.

Mutton Surprise

Serves 4

Ingredients

1 kg mutton
2 onions, *finely chopped*
4 tomatoes, *finely chopped*
1½ tsp cumin seeds
250 gm kidney beans
100 gm mushrooms, *chopped*
2 tbsp self-raising flour
2 tbsp ghee
A few chopped coriander leaves
for garnishing
Salt and pepper to taste

Method

1. Soak the beans overnight.
2. Cut the meat into small pieces.
3. Mix the flour well with the meat pieces.
4. Heat the ghee, add the cumin seeds and let then splutter. Add the onions and fry till they turn pink.
5. Add the chopped tomatoes and mushrooms and stir well.
6. Then add the meat pieces and cook till half done.
7. Add the beans, 1 cup water and salt and pepper. Cover with a lid and cook for about 1½ hours, or till done.
8. Serve hot, garnished with the chopped coriander leaves.

Mutton Korma

Serves 4

<u>Ingredients</u>

¼ kg mutton
1 cup grated coconut
2 tomatoes, chopped
½ cup onion-ginger-garlic paste
10-12 each of cloves, cinnamon and cardamoms
4 each of red and green chillies, chopped
2 tsp curd
A few curry leaves
2 tbsp oil
1 tbsp each of coriander and mint leaves
Salt and turmeric powder to taste

Method

1. Mix the coconut with the onion-ginger-garlic paste.
2. Grind together the cloves, cardamoms, cinnamon, mint leaves and coriander leaves to a paste.
3. Cut the mutton into small pieces. Add turmeric powder and cook till done.
4. Heat the oil in a separate pan and fry the paste till it turns brown.
5. Add the tomatoes and curry leaves.
6. Add salt and the red chillies and green chillies. Stir well.
7. Then pour the curd into the mixture.
8. Add the mutton pieces and cook for 5-10 minutes.
9. Serve hot.

Mutton Macaroni

Serves 5

Ingredients

½ kg mutton, cut into 1" pieces
100 gm macaroni
1 cup curd
2 tbsp lemon juice
4 tsp chilli powder
1 tsp turmeric powder
2 tsp ginger-garlic paste
4 onions, chopped
Oil
Coriander leaves for garnishing
Salt to taste

Method

1. Saute the onions in 2 tbsp oil till they turn pink in colour.
2. Rub the ginger-garlic paste and salt into the mutton pieces and marinate for 15-20 minutes.
3. Mix the curd, ½ tsp turmeric powder, 2 tsp chilli powder and the mutton pieces in it. Keep aside for another 30 minutes.
4. Fry these pieces with the sauted onions. When the meat becomes tender, add the macaroni.
5. Add 1 cup water, a pinch of salt and the remaining chilli and turmeric powders. Lower the flame. Cook for about 10-12 minutes, or till the macaroni is done.
6. Add the lemon juice before serving and toss well. Garnish with the chopped coriander leaves.

Pumpkin Mutton Korma

Serves 6

Ingredients

250 gm mutton
500 gm red pumpkin
150 gm curd
4 onions, chopped
2 tsp garam masala
2 tsp garlic-ginger-green chilli paste
1 bay leaf
Oil
2 tsp coriander leaves, chopped
Salt, chilli and turmeric powder to taste

Method

1. Cut the mutton into small pieces. Mix the curd and salt and smear on the mutton pieces. Marinate the mutton for an hour.
2. Heat the oil and fry the onions till pink. Add the garlic-ginger-green chilli paste and fry till golden brown.
3. Add turmeric, chilli powder, salt and the garam masala, bay leaf, green chillies and then the mutton pieces along with the curd. Saute till it becomes brown.
4. Then add 1 cup water and cook till the mutton is tender. Remove from the fire.
5. Peel and boil the red pumpkin, and mash it well.
6. Add this to the mutton and cook till the gravy thickens.
7. Garnish with the chopped coriander leaves. Serve hot.

Tamarind Meat Curry

Serves 4

Ingredients

1 kg meat, cut into pieces
½ cup oil
½ cup tamarind pulp
2 tbsp ginger-garlic paste
1 tsp turmeric powder
10-11 green chillies
1 bunch mint leaves
1 bunch coriander leaves
4 onions, sliced
Salt and chilli powder to taste

Method

1. Rub the meat with the garlic-ginger paste, turmeric and chilli powder and salt. Keep aside for 2 hours.
2. Grind together the green chillies, mint and coriander leaves. Add the tamarind pulp to it.
3. Heat the oil and fry the onions till translucent (keep some aside for garnishing).
4. Add the meat and fry for 5-7 minutes. Then add 1 cup water and cover with a lid.
5. Cook over a low flame till the meat is tender. Serve hot with parathas.

Mango Gosht

Serves 4

Ingredients

1 kg meat, cut into pieces
¼ kg raw green mangoes, peeled and cut into strips
¼ kg onions, sliced
2 tbsp ginger-garlic paste
½ tsp turmeric powder
½ cup oil
1 cup water
Coriander leaves for garnishing
Salt and chilli powder to taste

Method

1. Wash the meat, rub the ginger-garlic paste, turmeric and salt and chilli powder on it. Keep aside for an hour.
2. Heat the oil and fry the onion till it turns pink in colour.
3. Add the meat and fry till it is brown.
4. Add 1 cup of water and cook over a low flame till the meat is tender.
5. Add the mangoes to the meat and cook for 5-10 minutes, stirring all the while.
6. Cook till done. Garnish with the coriander leaves.

Cabbage Gosht

Serves 5

Ingredients

1 kg meat, washed and chopped
1 cabbage, shredded
½ cup curd
½ cup water
4 onions, sliced
2 tbsp oil
1 tbsp ginger-garlic paste
Coriander leaves for garnishing
Salt and chilli powder to taste

Method

1. Mix the curd, ginger-garlic paste and salt and chilli powder. Marinate the meat in it. Keep aside for 30-35 minutes.
2. Heat the oil, fry the sliced onions till brown.
3. Add the marinated meat. Fry for 5-10 minutes, then add ½ cup water and cover with a lid.
4. Lower the flame and cook till the meat is tender.
5. Add the cabbage. Lower the flame and cook till the cabbage is done.
6. Serve garnished with the coriander leaves.

Meat Loaf

Serves 4

Ingredients

1 kg meat, ground
½ onion, grated
1 egg, beaten
¾ cup breadcrumbs
1 cup tomato juice
1 tbsp soya sauce
Salt and pepper to taste

Method

1. Mix well the meat, onion, soya sauce, breadcrumbs, tomato juice, and salt and pepper.
2. Add the beaten egg and whisk well.
3. Grease a loaf tin and pour the mixture into it.
4. Bake in a hot oven (350^0C) till the loaf is done.

Potato Meat Curry

Serves 4

Ingredients

1 kg meat
4 potatoes, peeled and diced
½ cup curd
4 onions, sliced
2 tsp ginger-garlic paste
2 tbsp oil
2 cups water
Chopped coriander leaves for garnishing
Salt and chilli powder to taste

Method

1. Wash the meat and cut into cubes.
2. Rub a little salt on the pieces and keep aside for 1½ hours.
3. Mix together the ginger-garlic paste, curd and salt and chilli powder.
4. Heat the oil, add the onions and fry till pink in colour.
5. Add the curd-spice mixture and fry for 2-3 minutes, stirring all the while.
6. Add 1 cup water and the meat pieces. Stir well. Lower the flame and cook till the meat is tender.
7. Add the potatoes to the meat together with the remaining water. Cook till the potatoes are done.
8. Garnish with the chopped coriander leaves and serve hot.

Mutton Beetroot Curry

Serves 6

Ingredients

½ kg mutton, cut into 1" cubes
6 medium-sized beetroots, peeled and diced
1½ cups finely sliced onions
3 tsp minced ginger
3 tsp minced garlic
4 tsp coriander powder
4 tsp cumin powder
1 tsp turmeric powder
½ tsp chilli powder
1 tsp garam masala
6 tbsp oil
3½ cups water
Salt to taste

Method

1. Heat the oil and fry the onions till golden brown in colour.
2. Add the garlic and ginger and stir fry for a minute.
3. Put in all the dry ingredients and fry for 3-4 minutes.
4. Add the meat cubes and fry until the meat is lightly browned. Remove the meat and set aside.
5. Stir in the beetroots and fry for 2 minutes.
6. Add 3½ cups water and bring to the boil.
7. Lower the flame and cook until the meat is tender and dry. Serve hot.

Meat Koftas

Serves 4

Ingredients

1 kg meat, minced
4 cups meat stock
1 cup milk
2 eggs, beaten
½ cup breadcrumbs
4 spring onions, chopped
Oil for deep frying
2 tbsp chopped coriander leaves and green chillies
Coriander leaves for garnishing
Salt and chilli powder to taste

Method

1. Whisk the eggs with the meat.
2. Add the onions, chillies, coriander leaves and breadcrumbs to it.
3. Add salt and chilli powder.
4. Knead into a smooth dough.
5. Heat the oil. Shape spoonfuls of the mixture into small round balls and deep fry till golden brown. Keep aside.
6. In a pan, pour the meat stock and milk.
7. Add the meat balls to it and cook for 15-20 minutes.
8. Garnish with the coriander leaves. Serve hot.

Keema Matar

Serves 4

Ingredients

½ kg meat, minced
1 cup corn oil
1 cup sliced onions
½ kg green peas
2 tbsp ginger-garlic paste
½ tsp turmeric powder
Coriander leaves for garnishing
Salt and chilli powder to taste

Method

1. Mix the minced meat, turmeric powder, ginger-garlic paste and salt and chilli powder. Keep aside for 30-35 minutes.
2. Heat the oil, fry the onions till translucent.
3. Add the meat to it. Add ½ cup hot water and cook till the meat is tender and the water is nearly dried up.
4. Add the green peas and 1 tsp salt. Cook till the peas are tender.
5. Garnish with the coriander leaves and serve hot.

Mince Samosa

Serves 4

Ingredients

½ kg meat, minced
2 cups self-raising flour
1 onion, sliced
1 tbsp grated ginger-garlic
3 chopped green chillies
2 ½ cups oil
1 cup water
Salt and chilli powder to taste ·

Method

1. Heat 2 tbsp oil, fry the onion till pink.
2. Add the ginger-garlic paste. Fry for 5-10 minutes, or till they turn pink.
3. Add the meat, green chillies and salt and chilli powder. Add 1 cup water. Cook till the meat is tender and the water dries up.
4. Sift the flour with 1 tsp salt. Add the oil and enough water to make a stiff dough.
5. Shape into small round balls and roll out on the board. Cut each into two halves. Make a cone of each and fill the meat mixture into it. Press and seal the sides.
6. Deep fry in the hot oil. Serve hot with tomato ketchup.

Stuffed Cabbage Rolls

Serves 7

Ingredients

½ kg meat, minced
10 large cabbage leaves
1 onion, sliced
1 cup oil
1 cup water
Salt and chilli powder to taste

Method

1. Blanch the cabbage leaves in salted water for 3-4 minutes. Drain and keep aside.
2. Heat 2 tbsp oil, fry the onion till pink in colour.
3. Add the meat and salt and chilli powder.
4. Add the water and cook till the meat is tender and the water dries up.
5. Take a cabbage leaf and place some of this mixture in the centre. Fold its edges from all sides and tie with a thread.
6. Pour 2 tbsp oil in a frying pan and fry these cabbage rolls. When light golden in colour on one side, turn it over and fry the other side. Add more oil for frying the other rolls.
7. Serve hot with tomato ketchup.

Mughlai Keema

Serves 4

Ingredients

½ kg meat, minced
4 onions, sliced
3 tomatoes, chopped
4-5 green chillies, chopped
2 tbsp ginger-garlic paste
½ bunch spinach and fenugreek
leaves, chopped
2 tbsp oil
1 tbsp coriander leaves, chopped
Salt, chilli and turmeric powder to taste

Method

1. Wash and squeeze the meat to remove the water.
2. Heat the oil and fry the onions.
3. Season with salt, chilli powder and turmeric powder.
4. Add the ginger-garlic paste and fry well.
5. Add the tomatoes and stir well.
6. Then add the meat and fry for 5-10 minutes.
7. Add the spinach and fenugreek leaves. Cook till dry.
8. Garnish with the green chillies and coriander leaves before serving.

Mughlai Paratha

Serves 4

Ingredients

½ kg meat, minced
2 cups flour
100 gm butter
2 tsp sugar
3 eggs
3 onions
4 tbsp ghee
½ cup oil
2 tsp salt

Method

1. Knead the flour, sugar, butter and salt, with a little water into a soft dough.
2. Cut the onions into rings. Make 3 omelettes and then cut them into 3 pieces each. Keep them aside.
3. Fry the meat in the oil till brown and then pressure cook till tender.
4. Divide the dough into small portions. Then shape into balls. Roll out on a board and put some meat over it. Then place the onion rings on top of it, followed by one piece of an omelette. Cover with another rolled-out dough and seal the edges.
5. Fry over a medium flame, using a little ghee, till both sides turn brown in colour.

Stuffed Tomatoes

Serves 5

Ingredients

½ kg meat, minced
6 large tomatoes
1 chopped onion
1 tbsp ginger, chopped
1 tbsp coriander leaves, chopped
3 green chillies, chopped
2 tbsp oil
Salt and red chilli powder to taste

Method

1. Wash and dry the tomatoes. Cut them into equal halves. Scoop out the inside and place them upside down.
2. Heat 1 tsp oil and fry the onion and ginger till pink.
3. Add the green chillies and fry for another 2 minutes. Then add the meat and salt and chilli powder. Cook till it is tender and dry.
4. When it is cool, add the coriander leaves and mix well.
5. Stuff this mixture in the tomatoes.
6. Bake in a moderate oven (150^0C) for 5-10 minutes. Serve hot.

Pineapple Meatballs

Serves 3-4

Ingredients

½ kg steak, minced
1 clove garlic, crushed
¼ cup breadcrumbs
1 tsp Worcestershire sauce
½ tsp tabasco sauce
2 cups oil
Flour for dusting
Coriander leaves for garnishing
½ kg canned pineapple

Method

1. Mix well the steak, tabasco and Worcestershire sauces, garlic and breadcrumbs.
2. Shape them into balls. Roll into the flour and deep fry till golden brown.
3. While serving, top each meatball with a pineapple piece, using a toothpick. Serve with tomato ketchup.

Lentil Meat Curry

Serves 4-5

Ingredients

½ kg meat, minced
5 tomatoes, chopped
1 cup lentil
2 cups water
3 onions, chopped
1 tbsp ginger-garlic paste
2 tbsp oil
Coriander leaves for garnishing
Salt and chilli powder to taste

Method

1. Boil the lentil in the water till done.
2. Heat the oil. Saute the onions till pink, then add the ginger-garlic paste and fry for 4-5 minutes.
3. Add the tomatoes and stir till it forms a gravy.
4. Then add the meat and fry till brown.
5. Add the lentil and salt and chilli powder. Cover and cook till well done.
6. Serve hot, garnished with the chopped coriander leaves.

Eggplant Meat

Serves 5-6

Ingredients

1 kg meat, minced
5 eggplants, cut into 4 cubes each
4 onions
1 tbsp ginger-garlic paste
1 walnut-sized tamarind ball
Coriander leaves for garnishing
2 tbsp oil
Salt and red chilli powder to taste

Method

1. Soak the tamarind in hot water.
2. Wash the meat, apply the ginger-garlic paste and salt and red chilli powder to it. Keep aside for 15-20 minutes.
3. Heat the oil, fry the onions till pink, then add the meat and fry till tender.
4. Add the eggplants and tamarind pulp.
5. Cover with a lid and cook over a low flame till done.
6. Serve hot, garnished with the coriander leaves.

Meat with Lady's Fingers

Serves 4-5

Ingredients

1 kg meat, minced
½ kg lady's fingers
4 onions, sliced
1 tsp ginger-garlic paste
4 green chillies
1 bunch mint leaves
1 tbsp oil
1 bunch coriander leaves
Salt and chilli powder to taste

Method

1. Heat the oil and fry the onions till translucent.
2. Add the ginger-garlic paste and fry for another 5-10 minutes.
3. Add the meat and salt and chilli powder.
4. Add 1 cup water and cook till the meat is tender.
5. Cut the lady's fingers into halves lengthwise.
6. Add this to the pan and cook over a low flame till done.
7. Garnish with the coriander leaves. Serve hot with parathas.

Stuffed Capsicums

Serves 6

Ingredients

½ kg meat, minced
6 capsicums
2 cups grated onions
2 tomatoes, chopped
2 tbsp ginger-garlic paste
3 tsp coriander powder
1 tsp cumin powder
½ tsp each of garam masala and turmeric powder
2 green chillies, chopped
2 tbsp coriander leaves, chopped
½ cup oil

Method

1. Fry the onions in ¼ cup oil till translucent. Add the ginger-garlic paste and fry for a minute.
2. Stir in all the powders, green chillies and coriander leaves and stir-fry for a few minutes.
3. Add the tomatoes and fry for 3-5 minutes. Add the meat and fry till brown.
4. Slice the top of the capsicums and reserve them. Scoop out the seeds and mix with the mince.
5. Stuff the capsicums with the meat mixture, and replace the capsicum tops to seal them.
6. Heat the remaining oil in a pan. Add the capsicums and fry for about 5 mins.
7. Remove and drain on an absorbent paper. Serve hot with any sauce or dip.

Mutton Biryani with Carrots

Serves 6

Ingredients

1 kg mutton
½ cup each of curd and grated corrots
4 potatoes, cut into rounds slices
6 onions, 3 cloves
3 tbsp ginger-garlic paste
2 tbsp ghee, ½ tsp saffron
3 cups rice, 2 bay leaves
1 tsp garam masala
2 tbsp each of milk and oil
1 tbsp rose water
2 tbsp each of cardamom-cinnamon and chilli powder
Salt to taste

Method

1. Boil water. Add the cardamom-cinnamon powder, bay leaves, cloves and salt.
2. Add the rice and cook till half done. Drain the water and keep aside.
3. Heat the oil and fry the onions and ginger-garlic paste till pink.
4. Then add the garam masala, chilli powder and chopped tomatoes and salt. Stir well.
5. Add the curd and cook till it forms a gravy-like consistency.
6. Add the mutton pieces and cook till tender. Remove from the fire.
7. Deep fry the potatoes.
8. Pour the ghee into a pan. Then spread 3-4 tbsp rice followed by a layer of mutton and fried potatoes over it. Repeat the

same till all is consumed (the rice should be the topmost layer).

9. Dissolve the saffron in milk and sprinkle it all over the rice.
10. Add the rose water for flavour. Cover with a lid and cook till the rice is done.
11. Garnish with the grated carrot and serve hot.

Lamb

Lamb Loaf

Serves 5

Ingredients

1 kg minced lamb
2 eggs, well beaten
1 cup milk
2-3 bread slices, cut into small pieces
1 onion
2 cloves garlic
½" piece ginger
2 tbsp chopped coriander and
green chillies
Hard boiled eggs and tomatoes for
garnishing
Salt and pepper to taste

Method

1. Add the milk and bread pieces to the eggs.
2. Chop the onion, garlic and ginger. Add to the minced meat.
3. Add the coriander, chillies and salt and pepper. Blend well with the egg mixture.
4. Grease a loaf tin and pour the mixture into it. Bake in a moderate oven (150°C) till done.
5. When it is done, transfer to a plate.
6. Garnish with the slices of hard-boiled eggs and tomatoes.

Lamb Kebabs

Serves 4

Ingredients

½ kg lamb fillets
100 gm button mushrooms, washed
1 tsp turmeric powder
1 tsp paprika
2 tbsp white vinegar
1 tbsp lemon juice
2 bay leaves
Salt and pepper to taste

Method

1. Cut the lamb fillets into 1" cubes.
2. In a bowl, mix the turmeric, paprika, vinegar, lemon juice, bay leaves and salt and pepper.
3. Add the lamb pieces to this and marinate for 3-4 hours, turning the pieces over from time to time.
4. Thread the lamb pieces on to skewers, alternating the button mushrooms with the lamb pieces.
5. Grill for about 10 minutes, or till the meat is browned and cooked. Serve hot.

Cauliflower Lamb

Serves 5

Ingredients

½ kg cauliflower, cut into florets
½ kg lamb
2 onions
1" piece each of ginger and garlic
1 tbsp grated ginger-garlic
2 tomatoes, chopped
1 tsp garam masala
1 tsp each of coriander, turmeric and
chilli powder
2 cups water
2 tbsp each of ghee and curd
Chopped coriander leaves for garnishing
Salt to taste

Method

1. Wash the meat and cut into 1" pieces.
2. Grind the onions, ginger and garlic together and fry in the ghee.
3. When it turns pink, add the chopped tomatoes and cook for 4-5 minutes.
4. Add the curd, chilli powder, garam masala, turmeric and coriander powder and salt. Stir till the curd mixes well.
5. Add the meat pieces and 1 cup water. Cook for 20-25 minutes.
6. Add the cauliflower pieces and stir well. Add the remaining water, cover with a lid and cook till the cauliflower and meat are tender.
7. Garnish with the chopped coriander leaves before serving.

Lamb Curry

Serves 5

Ingredients

½ kg lamb, cut into cubes
3 onions, sliced
2 cloves garlic, crushed
½ tsp each of cinnamon and cardamom powder
½ tsp coriander seeds
1 tsp shredded ginger
1 tsp lemon juice
100 gm green peas
1 cup curd
2 tbsp oil
Chopped coriander leaves for garnishing
Salt and chilli powder to taste

Method

1. Heat the oil, fry the onions, garlic and ginger till light brown in colour.
2. Add the lamb cubes and cook till tender.
3. Pour the curd and stir till it mixes well.
4. Add the spices, lemon juice, green peas and salt and chilli powder.
5. Add a little water and cover with a lid.
6. Lower the flame and cook till done.
7. Garnish with the chopped coriander leaves and serve hot.

Lamb Chops

Serves 5

Ingredients

6-8 large lamb chops
4-5 cloves garlic, crushed
2 large potatoes, sliced
1 cup oil
1 cup curd
2 eggs, beaten
1 tsp lemon juice
1 tsp chilli powder
1 tsp garam masala
Salt and pepper to taste

Method

1. Mix together the garlic, garam masala, curd, lemon juice and salt and pepper.
2. Smear the lamb chops with this mixture and marinate for over an hour.
3. Dip the chops into the beaten eggs and deep fry till brown.
4. Fry the potato slices.
5. Serve hot with tomato sauce and the potato fries.

Lamb Tongue Curry

Serves 5

Ingredients

4 lamb tongues, washed and cut into pieces
4 onions, sliced
½ cup curd
2 tsp poppy seeds
2 tsp grated coconut
4-5 almonds
2 tsp each of sesame and
coriander seeds
2 tsp garlic-ginger paste
2 tbsp oil
1 cup water
Coriander leaves for garnishing
Turmeric, salt and chilli powder to taste

Method

1. Dry roast the poppy, coriander and sesame seeds and almonds and coconut in a frying pan. When cool, grind them together with 2 tbsp water to form a paste.
2. Mix the curd, ginger-garlic paste and salt, turmeric and chilli powder. Mix together both the paste. Marinate the tongue pieces with this paste and leave for 25-30 minutes.
3. Heat the oil, add the sliced onions and fry till brown.
4. Add the tongue pieces along with the marinade, paste and 1 cup water. Cover and cook for about 15-20 minutes, or till tender.
5. Serve hot, garnished with the chopped coriander leaves.

Minced Lamb Khichdi

Serves 6

Ingredients

1 kg minced lamb
4 cups rice
1 cup each of milk and curd
4 onions, fried
2 tbsp ginger-garlic paste
½ tsp turmeric powder
2 tsp cumin seeds
1 tsp sesame seeds, roasted
4-5 cardamoms
½" piece cinnamon
2-3 cloves
2-3 tsp poppy seeds, roasted
1 tsp grated coconut
½ cup oil
Salt to taste

Method

1. Grind together the roasted sesame seeds, poppy seeds, cumin seeds and turmeric powder and salt.
2. Add the curd to it and make a paste.
3. Heat the oil and fry the curd paste till it turns brown in colour.
4. Add the minced meat and cook till tender.
5. Boil the rice with the cinnamon, cloves and cardamoms till half done.
6. Then arrange a layer of meat over the rice.
7. Add the coconut and milk. Cover with a lid and cook over a low flame till the rice is done.
8. Decorate with the fried onions.

Lamb Rice Curry

Serves 4

Ingredients

1 kg lamb, cut into pieces
½ kg rice, washed
4 onions, cut into slices
½ cup oil
2 tbsp ginger-garlic paste
1 tsp cumin seeds
1 tsp poppy seeds
1 tsp sesame seeds
1 tsp grated coconut
Coriander leaves for garnishing
Salt and chilli powder to taste

Method

1. Mix together the ginger-garlic paste and salt and chilli powder. Smear the meat pieces with the paste. Keep aside for 2½-3 hours.
2. Heat a pan and dry roast the cumin seeds, poppy seeds, sesame seeds, coconut and rice till brown. When cool powder them.
3. Heat the oil and fry the onions till they turn pink.
4. Then add the rice-spice powder to the meat and fry till brown.
5. Add 2 cups water, cover and cook till the oil separates.
6. Serve hot, garnished with the chopped coriander leaves.

Lamb Cakes

Serves 4

Ingredients

1 kg minced lamb
4 cups semolina
2 cups butter
½ cup honey
½ cup water
4 onions
2 tbsp lemon juice
2 tbsp tomato sauce
1 tbsp ginger-garlic paste
1 bunch coriander leaves, chopped
1 bunch mint leaves, chopped
4-5 green chillies, chopped
½ tsp turmeric powder
Salt and chilli powder to taste

Method

1. Wash the meat.
2. Mix the ginger-garlic paste, turmeric powder and salt and chilli powder with the minced meat.
3. Heat 1 cup butter and fry the onions.
4. Add the meat and fry for 15-20 minutes. Add ½ cup water, cover and cook till the meat is tender. Let the water evaporate.
5. Remove from the fire and add the lemon juice.
6. Add the chopped green chillies, mint leaves and coriander leaves to the minced meat.
7. Pour the tomato sauce in it and stir well.
8. Mix together the remaining butter and semolina and knead into a soft dough.

9. Take a little dough, make small oval-shaped patties, filling them with the minced meat mixture.
10. Place all the patties on a tray and brush them with the honey.
11. Place them in a baking tin and cover with foil. Bake in a moderate oven (190°C) till the patties turn brown in colour.
12. Remove the foil and serve hot with mint chutney.

Chicken

Chinese Chicken

Serves 4

Ingredients

1 kg chicken, cut into pieces
5 onions, sliced
3 potatoes
3 tomatoes, chopped
1½ cups curd
1½ tbsp butter
1 tsp each of soya sauce, ajinomoto and garam masala powder
1 tsp each of chilli, cumin and coriander powder
½ tsp turmeric powder
1 cup oil
Coriander leaves for garnishing
Salt to taste

Method

1. Mix together the turmeric, garam masala, chilli, cumin and coriander powders, curd, ajinomoto, soya sauce and salt. Apply this on the chicken pieces and leave to marinate for 3-4 hours.

2. Heat the oil and fry the onions till brown. Remove and keep aside.

3. Peel the potatoes and cut them into long strips, then deep fry them.

4. In the same pan, add the marinated chicken, chopped tomatoes and sauce. Stir well.

5. Add ½ cup water and let it cook for 15-20 minutes, or till the chicken is tender. Add the butter and mix well.

6. Add the fried onion slices and potato. Serve hot, garnished with the chopped coriander leaves.

Tandoori Chicken

Serves 5

Ingredients

1½ kg chicken, cut into pieces
2 tbsp lemon juice
1 tsp honey
2" piece ginger
4 cloves garlic
2 green chillies
½ tsp garam masala
½ tsp fenugreek powder
½ cup curd
¾ tsp chilli powder
4 tbsp oil
Tomato, onion and lemon slices
for garnishing
Chat masala to taste
Salt to taste

Method

1. Grind the ginger, garlic and green chillies to a paste.
2. Mix the honey, lemon juice, garam masala, fenugreek leaves, curd, and chilli powder and salt. Apply it on the chicken pieces and marinate for 4-5 hours.
3. Then wrap the chicken pieces in aluminium foils and bake for 30-35 minutes.
4. Remove from the foil, glaze with the oil and bake again for 5-10 minutes.
5. Sprinkle chat masala.
6. Serve garnished with the tomato, onion and lemon slices.

Chicken Korma

Serves 4

Ingredients

1 chicken, cut into pieces
2 onions
1 tbsp ginger-garlic paste
1 tbsp coriander seeds
2 tsp cardamom-cinnamon powder
6 cloves
1 cup curd
2 tbsp oil
2 green chillies, chopped
Coriander leaves for garnishing
Salt and chilli powder to taste

Method

1. Grind one onion, green chillies and coriander seeds together. Add the ginger-garlic paste to it and mix well. Rub it on the chicken pieces along with salt and chilli powder and marinate.
2. Chop the other onion and fry it in the oil.
3. Add the cloves, cardamom-cinnamon powder and the marinated chicken pieces and fry for a while.
4. Add the curd, a little at a time, and stir well to avoid formation of lumps.
5. Cover and cook till done. Garnish with the coriander leaves.

Chicken Safeda

Serves 5

__Ingredients__

1 kg chicken, cut into pieces
1½ cups curd
½ cup groundnuts
¼ cup poppy seeds
1 tbsp coriander leaves
8 green chillies, chopped
1 tsp sugar
1 cup ghee
Salt to taste

Method

1. Grind the groundnuts and poppy seeds to a paste.
2. Add the curd to the paste. Add salt and the sugar and marinate the chicken pieces in this paste for 1-2 hours.
3. Heat the ghee in a vessel and fry the chicken pieces till brown in colour (add the marinade along with the pieces).
4. Then add the green chillies and cook over a low flame till done.
5. Garnish with the chopped coriander leaves. Serve hot.

Chicken Salad

Serves 5

Ingredients

½ kg chicken, cut into pieces
2 cups mayonnaise
1 cup walnut, crushed
1 bunch seedless grapes
4 eggs, hard-boiled and sliced
1 cup water
1 bunch celery
A few lettuce leaves
Salt and pepper to taste

Method

1. Cook the chicken in the water with salt and pepper. When tender, remove from the fire and cool.
2. Then add the mayonnaise, walnuts, grapes and celery and mix well.
3. Serve on a bed of lettuce leaves.
4. Garnish with the slices of hard-boiled eggs.

Chicken in Red Sauce

Serves 4

Ingredients

1½ kg chicken pieces
2 tbsp ginger-garlic paste
6 red onions, finely grated
2 tbsp lemon juice
1 tbsp butter
2 tbsp gin
1 cup tomato sauce
8 red chillies, ground to a paste
2 tbsp oil
Salt and sugar to taste

Method

1. Marinate the chicken in 1 tsp lemon juice for about an hour. Then rub it well with the butter and salt and roast till golden brown.
2. Heat the oil in a pan and add the onions and ginger-garlic paste.
3. When it turns pink, add the red chilli paste and stir for 2-3 minutes. Then add sugar and pour the lemon juice and tomato sauce. Mix well.
4. Allow to simmer till the gravy thickens. Add the gin.
5. Pour this sauce over the roasted chicken and serve with potato chips.

Chicken Pasanda

Serves 4

Ingredients

1½ kg chicken, cut into big cubes
3 onions, sliced
½ cup curd
1 tbsp ginger-garlic paste
1 tsp each of garam masala and chilli powder
2 tsp dry coconut, grated
6-8 almonds
1 tsp each of white sesame and poppy seeds
2 tbsp oil
Coriander leaves for garnishing
Salt to taste

Method

1. Mix the curd, ginger-garlic paste, chilli powder and garam masala and salt.
2. Apply this on the chicken pieces and leave to marinate for 25-30 minutes.
3. Grind the almonds, poppy seeds and sesame seeds to a paste.
4. Heat the oil in a wok and fry the onions along with the grated coconut. Cook till the onions turn translucent.
5. Add the marinated chicken and the marinade.
6. Add ½ cup water if desired. Lower the flame, cook till done. Garnish with the chopped coriander leaves.

Chicken Roast

Serves 4

Ingredients

1½ kg chicken pieces
1 cup breadcrumbs
2 tbsp butter
1 cup celery, chopped
6 eggs, beaten
1 tsp paprika
Coriander leaves for garnishing
Celery salt, garlic salt and pepper
to taste

Method

1. Boil the chicken in enough water till tender. Reserve 1 cup of the stock.
2. Heat the butter and add the breadcrumbs, stirring constantly. Remove from the fire.
3. Now mix the breadcrumbs, chopped celery, beaten eggs, paprika and salt and pepper. Add the chicken stock.
4. Heat a pan, put the chicken pieces in it. Cover with the breadcrumb mixture and bake in a moderate oven (150°C) till it turns golden brown.
5. Garnish with the coriander leaves and serve hot.

Saucy Chicken Feast

Serves 5

Ingredients

1 kg chicken pieces
2 cups curd
2 tbsp ginger-garlic paste
1½ tsp poppy seeds
1 tsp coriander seeds
3 onions
1 tsp garam masala
½ tsp sugar
2 tbsp oil
Coriander leaves for garnishing
Salt and chilli powder to taste

Method

1. Grind together the poppy seeds, coriander seeds, onions, ginger-garlic paste and chilli powder, adding 1/2 cup of water to make a paste.
2. Add the curd to it and mix well. Apply it to the chicken and marinate.
3. Heat the ghee, add the garam masala and sugar. When the sugar turns brown, remove the vessel and cool.
4. Now add the marinated chicken, mix well and return the vessel to the fire.
5. Fry over a low flame and cook till the chicken is tender.
6. Serve hot, garnished with the coriander leaves.

Chicken in Onion Sauce

Serves 6

Ingredients

*1 kg chicken pieces
2 tbsp soya sauce
2 tbsp cornflour
1 tsp ajinomoto
2 tbsp vinegar
2 onions, grated
1 tbsp chilli powder
3 green chillies, chopped
Oil for deep frying
Coriander leaves for garnishing
Salt to taste*

Method

1. Mix together the vinegar, soya sauce, ajinomoto, chilli powder and salt. Marinate the chicken pieces in this mixture for 1½ hours.

2. Heat the oil and deep fry the chicken pieces over a medium flame till they turn brown.

3. Heat 1 tbsp oil in a separate pan, fry the onions and green chillies till they turn pink. Add a cup of water and sprinkle some salt.

4. Mix the cornflour in 2 tbsp water and add this mixture to the gravy.

5. Stir till the gravy thickens, lower the flame and let it simmer for 5-7 minutes.

6. Now pour this sauce over the chicken pieces. Garnish with the chopped coriander leaves and serve hot.

Garlic Chicken Salad

Serves 2

Ingredients

200 gm chicken
1 apple, cut into cubes
1 onion, chopped
2 cloves garlic, crushed
½ cup fresh bean sprouts
2 tbsp lemon juice
2 tbsp white vinegar
½ cup oil
Salt and pepper to taste

Method

1. Mix the white vinegar and lemon juice and salt. Marinate the chicken pieces in it for 1½-2 hours.
2. Fry the bean sprouts in 2 tbsp oil for 3-5 minutes. Then spread them in the serving bowl.
3. Mix the onion, garlic, apple and salt and pepper.
4. Deep fry the marinated chicken pieces and mix in the apple salad.
5. Add these to the beans in the serving bowl.
6. Decorate with lettuce leaves.

Paprika Chicken Bake

Serves 5

Ingredients

1 kg chicken
2 tsp paprika
1 onion
1 red chilli
2 green chillies
5-6 cloves garlic
1 tsp oil
Salt and pepper to taste

Method

1. Cut the chicken into small pieces.
2. Grind the onion, garlic, red and green chillies and mix them in 1 tsp oil. Apply this on the chicken pieces and marinate for an hour.
3. Add the paprika (leaving aside a few for garnishing) and salt and pepper with 1 cup water to it.
4. Bake in a moderate oven (200^0C) for 30-40 minutes or till the chicken is done.
5. Garnish with the paprika before serving.

Chicken Mushroom Bake

Serves 6

Ingredients

1 kg chicken
1 tsp lemon juice
2 onions, chopped
100 gm button mushrooms
1 tsp celery salt
1 tsp coriander seeds
1 green chilli, chopped
2 tbsp oil
Coriander leaves for garnishing
Salt and pepper to taste

Method

1. Mix the lemon juice with salt and rub it on the chicken pieces. Leave them to marinate for 2 hours.
2. Heat the oil and fry the onions. When they turn pink, add the mushrooms.
3. When the mushrooms turn brown, add the green chilli and mix well.
4. Then sprinkle the celery salt and the coriander seeds. Mix well. Let it cook for 5 minutes.
5. Place the marinated chicken pieces on the baking dish. Cover with the mushroom mixture, and bake in a moderate oven (190°C) for about 25-30 minutes.
6. Garnish with the chopped coriander leaves. Serve hot.

Chicken Vegetable Delight

Serves 4

Ingredients

1 kg chicken, cut into pieces
4 carrots, sliced
2 onions, sliced
100 gm button mushrooms
1 cup tomato juice
2 tbsp oil
2 cloves garlic, crushed
1 cup curd
Salt and pepper to taste

Method

1. Marinate the chicken pieces in the curd and salt for 2 hours.
2. Fry the onions in the oil till pink.
3. Add the carrots and mushrooms and cook till they turn brown.
4. Add the garlic and stir for a while.
5. Then add the marinated chicken pieces and fry till they brown on all sides.
6. Add the tomato juice and salt and pepper and stir for a while.
7. Cover and let it cook till the chicken is done.
8. Serve hot.

Spinach Chicken

Serves 5

Ingredients

1 kg chicken, cut into pieces
4 onions, grated
6 tomatoes, chopped
2 tbsp ginger-garlic paste
2 tbsp curd
¾ kg spinach, chopped
1 tsp cumin seeds
2 tbsp oil
1 tbsp cottage cheese, grated
Salt and chilli powder to taste

Method

1. In a bowl pour the curd and add salt and chilli powder. Marinate the chicken pieces in it for 2 hours.
2. Heat the oil and fry the cumin seeds. When they begin to splutter, add the onion and ginger-garlic paste.
3. When it turns pink, add the marinated pieces and fry for 4-5 minutes.
4. Then add the chopped tomatoes and stir well.
5. When the gravy thickens, add the spinach and sprinkle salt. Cook over a low flame till the spinach and chicken are done.
6. Garnish with the grated cottage cheese and serve hot.

Black Pepper Chicken

Serves 5

Ingredients

1 kg chicken, cut into pieces
1 cup curd
½ cup oil
Onion rings for garnishing
Salt and pepper to taste

Method

1. Apply the curd and some salt on the chicken pieces and marinate them for 2 hours.
2. Heat the oil and fry the marinated chicken pieces.
3. When golden brown, sprinkle salt and pepper.
4. Cook till done. Garnish with the onion rings. Serve with tomato sauce.

Chicken in Garlic Sauce

Serves 4

Ingredients

1 kg chicken, cut into pieces
1 onion, crushed
1 red chilli
3 tomatoes, chopped
100 gm baby mushrooms
5-6 cloves garlic, crushed
¼ cup red wine
2 tbsp oil
Coriander leaves for garnishing
Salt and chilli powder to taste

Method

1. Heat the oil and fry the onion and garlic till they turn pink in colour.
2. Add the tomatoes and stir till a gravy forms.
3. Add the mushrooms and cook for 5 minutes.
4. Then add the chicken pieces, red chilli and salt and chilli powder.
5. Bring it to the boil. Cover with a lid and cook till the chicken is done.
6. Serve garnished with the coriander leaves.

Chicken in Spicy Peanut Sauce

Serves 5

Ingredients

*1 kg chicken, cut into pieces
2 tbsp butter
1 tsp each of curry powder, grated ginger and honey
4 cloves garlic, crushed
½ cup roasted and ground peanuts
½ cup peanut butter
½ cup water
¼ cup cherry
¼ tsp tabasco sauce
Coriander leaves for garnishing
Salt to taste*

Method

1. Melt the butter, add the curry powder, garlic, ginger and peanuts. Stir well and cook for 2-3 minutes.
2. Mix the peanut butter, cherry, honey and tabasco sauce in a separate bowl. Pour the water into it and add to the above mixture.
3. Stir till it boils and then add the chicken pieces. Sprinkle salt.
4. Cook over a low flame till the chicken is tender.
5. Serve garnished with the chopped coriander leaves.

Chicken Coconut Delight

Serves 4

Ingredients

1 kg chicken pieces
2 cups curd
2 tbsp grated fresh coconut
1 tbsp garlic paste
3 onions
2 each of tomatoes, potatoes and red chillies
1 tsp garam masala powder
½ tsp sesame seeds
1 tbsp clove-cinnamon-cardamom powder
½ tsp cumin seeds
Oil
Salt and chilli powder to taste

Method

1. Mix the garlic paste, curd and salt and chilli powder. Apply this to the chicken pieces and marinate .

2. Bake the onions whole in a moderate oven (about $190^0\,C$) till well browned on all sides.

3. Heat 2 tbsp oil and fry the cumin seeds.

4. Then add the clove-clove-cinnamon-cardamom powder, sesame seeds and red chillies. Remove from the fire and let it cool.

5. Grind this masala along with the baked onions and 1 tbsp coconut to a fine paste.

6. In a pan, heat the oil and fry the marinated chicken pieces.

7. Add the paste, fry till the masala mixes well and turns brown.

8. Add the chopped tomatoes and saute for 5-10 minutes.
9. Then add the potatoes and garam masala powder and salt.
10. Cover and cook over a low flame till the potatoes and chicken are done.
11. Garnish with the remaining grated coconut and serve hot.

Fish and Seafood

Garlic Shrimps

Serves 4

Ingredients

½ kg shrimps, peeled
1 onion
3 cloves garlic
2 tomatoes
2 tbsp oil
Coriander leaves for garnishing
Salt and pepper to taste

Method

1. Chop the onion and tomatoes and crush the garlic.
2. Heat the oil and fry the onion and garlic till they turn pink.
3. Add the tomatoes and cook till done.
4. Then add the shrimps and salt and pepper and cover with a lid. Cook over a low flame till done.
5. Serve hot, garnished with the coriander leaves.

Capsicum Prawns

Serves 3

Ingredients

½ kg prawns, shelled and drained
1 capsicum
1 onion
1 clove garlic
4 tbsp dry white wine
1 cup tomato juice
50 gm dried apricots
2 tbsp oil
Salt and pepper to taste

Method

1. Chop the vegetables finely.
2. Heat the oil and fry the onion and garlic till pink in colour.
3. Then add the chopped capsicum and prawns and cook till tender.
4. Add the tomato juice, apricots and salt and pepper.
5. After 4-5 minutes, add the wine. Lower the flame, cover with a lid and let it cook for about 10 minutes.
6. Garnish with pepper and serve hot.

Sardine Egg Delight

Serves 4

Ingredients

½ kg meat, minced
1 small tin sardines
4 eggs
4-5 tbsp breadcrumbs
6 eggs, hard-boiled
2 cups oil
Salt, pepper and chilli powder to taste

Method

1. Cook the meat, cool and then mash it finely.
2. Chop the sardines and add to the meat.
3. Beat the eggs and add them to the meat-fish mixture along with the breadcrumbs and salt, pepper and chilli powder. Mix well.
4. Dip the hard-boiled eggs in this batter and coat well on all sides.
5. Deep fry in the hot oil.
6. Cut each egg half and serve hot.

Tuna Burgers/Sandwiches

Serves 4

Ingredients

1 can tuna fish
1 onion, chopped
¼ cup mayonnaise
½ cup cheese
1 cup chopped celery
12 slices hamburger rolls/bread
Salt and pepper to taste

Method

1. Mix the fish, onion, mayonnaise, celery, cheese and salt and pepper.
2. If using hamburger rolls, then butter the insides of the rolls. If using bread then butter the slices.
3. Apply the fish mixture liberally on the rolls/slices.
4. Wrap them in a foil. Bake in a moderate oven (150°C) for 15-20 minutes, or until done.

Oyster Fry

Serves 3

Ingredients

12 oysters
2 eggs
2 tbsp milk
1½ cups breadcrumbs
2 cups oil
1 cup onion rings

Method

1. Mix together the eggs and milk and beat the mixture well.
2. Dip the oysters into this mixture and then roll them in the breadcrumbs.
3. Deep fry the oysters in the hot oil till golden brown.
4. Fry the onion rings. Serve the oysters hot with tomato sauce and garnished with the onion rings.

Crab Curry

Serves 3

Ingredients

6 large crabs
½ cup grated fresh coconut
8 onions, chopped
8 each of peppercorns and cloves
1 tbsp coriander seeds
2 tsp chilli powder
1 tsp turmeric powder
½ tsp curry powder
2 tbsp each of oil and tamarind juice
Coriander leaves for garnishing
Salt to taste

Method

1. Heat the oil and fry the cloves, peppercorns and coriander seeds.
2. Add the onions and fry till golden brown in colour.
3. Add the coconut and fry till brown. Cool and grind to a paste.
4. Boil the crabs till the pincers are red.
5. Sprinkle salt and the chilli, turmeric and curry powders.
6. Add the coconut paste. Stir till it mixes well.
7. Then add the tamarind juice and let it cook till done.
8. Garnish with the coriander leaves.

Prawn Masala

Serves 5

Ingredients

2 cups prawns, shelled and drained
300 gm cauliflower florets
4 tomatoes, chopped
2 potatoes, cut into cubes
4 onions, chopped
1 tbsp coriander seeds
1 tsp garam masala
2 tsp chilli powder
1 tsp turmeric powder
2 tbsp coriander leaves
Salt to taste

Method

1. Wash the prawns well.
2. Heat the oil and fry the onions till pink.
3. Add the prawns and vegetables. Stir well.
4. After 4-5 minutes, add salt and the chilli powder, turmeric powder, garam masala and coriander seeds.
5. Add 1 cup water.
6. Cook till the prawns are tender.
7. Garnish with the chopped coriander leaves.

Shrimp Salad

Serves 3

Ingredients

250 gm shrimps, shelled and drained
2 cups mayonnaise
3 apples
1 bunch horse radish
Coriander leaves for garnishing
Salt and pepper to taste

Method

1. Boil the shrimps with salt.
2. Cut the horse radish into rings.
3. Peel and slice the apples.
4. Mix the apples, radish, shrimps, mayonnaise and salt and pepper.
5. Garnish with the chopped coriander leaves.

Fish Curry

Serves 3

Ingredients

250 gm fish fillets
4 tomatoes, chopped
2 tsp ginger-garlic paste
2 tsp chilli powder
1 tbsp coriander-cumin powder
1 tsp turmeric powder
2 tbsp oil
Coriander leaves for garnishing
Salt to taste

Method

1. Heat the oil, fry the ginger-garlic paste till brown.
2. Then add the tomatoes and stir till the gravy thickens.
3. Add the chilli powder, turmeric powder, coriander and cumin powder and salt. Mix well.
4. Meanwhile, fry the fish pieces in the oil. When they turn brown, remove from the pan and put them in the tomato gravy.
5. Garnish with the chopped coriander leaves and serve hot.

Fish with Lime Butter

Serves 6

Ingredients

6 salmon steaks
2 tbsp butter
100 gm butter
½ cup peppercorns, crushed
2 tbsp grated lime rind
2 tbsp lime juice
3-4 cloves garlic, crushed
2 tbsp oil
Salt to taste

Method

1. Oil both the sides of the fish steaks and add the crushed peppercorns.
2. Heat 2 tbsp butter and saute the fish steaks till tender.
3. Make the lime butter by mixing salt and the crushed garlic cloves, butter, grated lime rind and lime juice.
4. Refrigerate this butter and serve, when firm, with hot fish steaks.

Prawn Mayonnaise

Makes 1 cup

Ingredients

½ kg prawns, shelled and deveined
1 egg yolk
1 tbsp white vinegar
1 tsp grated lemon rind
2 tsp lemon juice
2 tsp tomato sauce
2 tbsp butter
½ cup refined oil
Salt to taste

Method

1. Heat the butter and fry the prawns till brown.
2. Mix the egg yolk, vinegar, lemon rind, lemon juice and tomato sauce.
3. Sprinkle salt and heat well. Add the prawns.
4. Put the mixture in a blender and blend.
5. Add the oil gradually while blending. Blend till the mixture is smooth and thick.
6. Serve with cutlets, or as dressing for any salad.

Spinach Fish

Serves 5

Ingredients

1 kg each of fish and spinach
4 onion, sliced
1 cup corn oil
2 tbsp ginger-garlic paste
2 tsp coriander powder
2 tsp cumin seeds
1 tsp each of chilli and turmeric powders
1 tbsp grated cheese
Salt to taste

Method

1. Wash the fish and cut into pieces.
2. Wash and finely chop the spinach.
3. Mix ½ cup oil with the ginger-garlic paste, chilli, turmeric and coriander powders and salt. Rub it on the fish pieces.
4. Heat the remaining oil, fry the sliced onions till pink.
5. Then add the fish and chopped spinach. Stir gently and add ½ cup hot water.
6. Sprinkle some more salt.
7. Cook over a low flame till done.
8. Garnish with the grated cheese before serving.

Lobster Salad

Serves 3

Ingredients

3 lobsters
½ cup honey
½ cup white wine
1 tsp ginger, grated
2 carrots
1 tsp cornflour
1 red chilli
2 tsp chilli sauce
Coriander leaves for garnishing
Salt to taste

Method

1. Devein the lobsters.
2. Mix the honey, wine, chilli sauce, ginger and then sprinkle salt. Pour half of this into a pan. Bring it to the boil, lower the flame and cook for 4-5 minutes.
3. Cut the carrots into long strips and boil them till tender. Then place the lobsters and carrots in a serving bowl. Pour the remaining honey mixture into the pan.
4. Mix the cornflour with a little water to make a smooth paste and add it to the pan. Stir till it boils and thickens.
5. Add the chilli mixture and pour this over the lobsters and carrots. Garnish with the coriander leaves and serve hot.

Other Titles in the Series
All You Wanted To Know About

- *Soups*
- *Barbeque*
- *Chocolate*
- *Mughlai*
- *Potato*
- *Salads*
- *Meat*
- *Chinese*
- *Dessert*
- *Pasta*
- *Cakes*
- *Seafood*

Vegetarian

- *Puddings & Desserts*
- *Low Calorie Cooking*
- *Delightful Soups*
- *Kebabs & Snacks*
- *Cuisines from the World*
- *Menus from the World*

For further information contact:
STERLING PUBLISHERS PVT. LTD.
A-59 Okhla Industrial Area, Phase-II,
New Delhi- 110020.
Tel: 26387070, 26386209
E-mail: ghai@nde.vsnl.net.in